W9-BGM-423

11497

Our American Family™

I Am Native American

Ana Sage

The Rosen Publishing Group's
PowerKids Press™
New York

Library Media Center
Builta Elementary School

For Tiffany Greyeyes

Published in 1997 by The Rosen Publishing Group, Inc.
29 East 21st Street, New York, NY 10010

Copyright © 1997 by The Rosen Publishing Group, Inc.

All rights reserved. No part of this book may be reproduced in any form without permission in writing from the publisher, except by a reviewer.

First Edition

Book Design: Erin McKenna

Photo Credits: Cover © Jeffrey Jay Foxx; photo illustration © Icon Comm/FPG International Corp.; p. 4 © Michael Kornafel/FPG International Corp.; p. 7 © Peter Gridley/FPG International Corp.; p. 8 © Ken Ross/FPG International Corp.; p. 11 © Grehan, Farrell/FPG International Corp.; p. 12 © Neil Nissing/FPG International Corp.; p. 15 © Mark Gubin/MIDWESTOCK; p. 16 © Lee Kuhn/FPG International Corp.; p. 19 © Michael Krasowitz/FPG International Corp.; p. 20 © George C. Hight/FPG International Corp.

Sage, Ana.
    I Am Native American / by Ana Sage.
        p.   cm. — (Our American Family)
    Includes index.
    ISBN 0-8239-5014-X
    1. Indians of North America—Juvenile literature. 2. Hopi Indians—Juvenile literature.
    I. Title. II. Series.
E77.4.S78 1997
970'.0049745—dc21   97-2468
                                                            CIP
                                                            AC

Manufactured in the United States of America

Contents

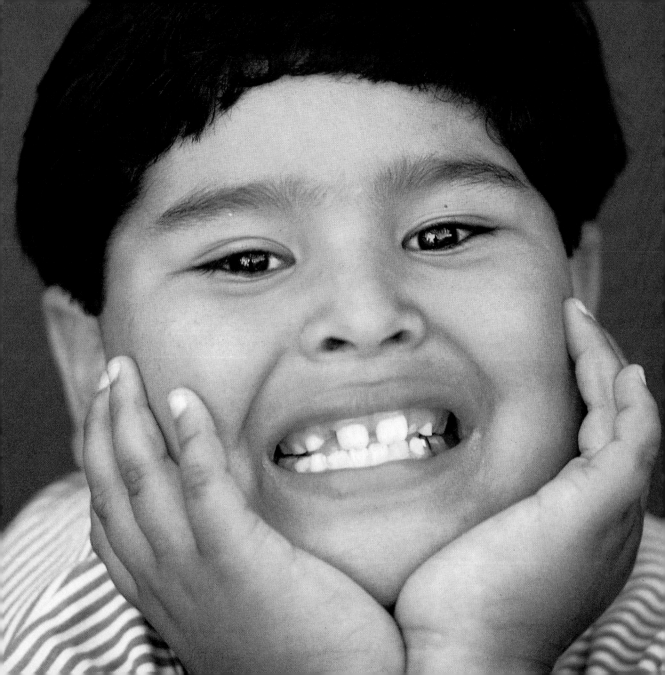

Austin

  My name is Austin Yellow Bear. My family belongs to a Native American **tribe** (TRYB) called Hopi, which means "peace." Native Americans are also called American Indians. We live in Arizona on a **reservation** (reh-zer-VAY-shun).

  There are hundreds of different Native American tribes. Each one has its own language and its own way of doing things. However, Native Americans also have many beliefs in common.

◀ Being an American Indian means being an important part of American history.

5

The First Americans

When explorer Christopher Columbus reached land in 1492, he thought he had found India. He called the people he met Indians. But these people were actually the first Americans. American Indians have probably been in America for more than 20,000 years! Many Europeans who came to America treated Native Americans badly. They forced some Native Americans to work for them, tried to change their religions, and started battles that hurt or killed many of them.

Christopher Columbus led the first Europeans into what is now the United States of America. ▶

Reservations

European settlers, and later the U.S. government, took the Native Americans' land away from them. The Native Americans were moved to reservations. A reservation is an area set aside by the government for Native Americans to live on. There we have not been able to live in our **traditional** (truh-DISH-un-ul) ways. Today, it still can be hard to live on reservations. Many don't have schools near-by, so kids have to travel a long way every day. And often there aren't enough jobs for the grown-ups on the reservations.

◀ The Hopi's neighbors, the Navajo, have part of their reservation in the Painted Desert of Arizona.

Pueblos

My family lives in a Hopi **pueblo** (PWEH-bloh) on a reservation. The pueblo is on a high, flat area of land called a **mesa** (MAY-suh). The houses in the pueblo are connected to each other in groups. Each house has a big opening in its roof. We can go inside by climbing a ladder to it.

The Hopi Indians were once surrounded by enemies. The pueblos were like forts. If an enemy tried to get into a house, a Hopi could pull the ladder into the house to keep the enemy out.

The homes in a pueblo ▶ are joined together.

10

Kachinas

Native Americans have a lot of respect for nature. We believe that if we treat nature well, it will give us what we need. In fact, even though we live in pueblos, we think of all the land around us as our home. Most Native American religions are based on the spirits found in nature. Hopis pray to spirits called **kachinas** (kah-CHEE-nuhz). We may ask a kachina to give us good health, or we may ask for rain so we can grow crops of corn, squash, and beans.

Kachina dolls are painted bright colors and are decorated with feathers. Each doll represents a different kachina spirit.

13

Wuwuchim

Each Native American tribe has special **ceremonies** (SEHR-eh-mohn-eez) to honor their spirits. In November, Hopis celebrate Wuwuchim, or the Hopi New Year. For several days, priests lead ceremonies that include songs, prayers, and dances. Together, these tell the Hopi story of how the world was created. The priests ask the kachinas for a good new year too. When I am older, I will learn how to dance and pray with other Hopi during Wuwuchim.

14

Many American Indians still perform traditional ceremonies today. ▶

Clothing

Everyone in my family has special ceremonial clothes made by my mother and grandmother. We all have moccasins, which are soft beaded boots made from animal skins. My sisters wear black mantas, which are heavy dresses that go down past their knees. They each have bracelets and necklaces made from silver and a blue-green stone called **turquoise** (TER-koyz). For some ceremonies we paint colored markings on our faces or bodies.

◀ Turquoise jewelry, such as these hair clips, are often worn with colorful clothes during Hopi ceremonies.

Corn

It is a Native American tradition to get all our food from nature. In the past, many tribes hunted and farmed for their food. My tribe still grows many crops, especially corn. In fact, we have more than twenty kinds of corn, which grow in all different colors. My grandmother makes a thin bread called piki out of cornmeal that she grinds from blue corn. Corn is such an important part of Hopi life that it's often part of our ceremonies.

Hopis often eat corn as a part of their meals. ▶

Crafts

Crafts are a very important part of the Native American tradition. Women and girls weave all kinds of baskets and rugs. The baskets and rugs are decorated with animal shapes or special colorful patterns. Boys and men make robes and masks that are used for ceremonies. Many Native Americans, including the Hopi, also make beautiful jewelry out of silver and turquoise.

◀ Animals are very important to many Native American tribes. This can be seen in our jewelry and crafts.

21

I Am Native American

Before Christopher Columbus and other Europeans arrived, Native Americans were the only people living in what is now called the United States. Today, many of the traditional Indian ways of life are gone. I know that we can only keep our **culture** (KUL-cher) alive if we honor the way our **ancestors** (AN-sesterz) lived. Most of the time, I wear jeans, eat pizza, and play sports with my friends. But I'll never forget the Hopi traditions. I am proud of my Native American **heritage** (HEHR-eh-tej).

22

Glossary

ancestor (AN-ses-ter) A relative who lived before you.

ceremony (SEHR-eh-mohn-ee) A special act that keeps the traditions of a culture alive.

culture (KUL-cher) The customs, art, and religion of a group of people.

heritage (HEHR-eh-tej) Cultural traditions that are handed down from parent to child.

kachina (kah-CHEE-nuh) A Hopi spirit. Some other tribes, like the Zuni, also honor kachinas.

mesa (MAY-suh) A flat area of land at the top of a tall hill.

pueblo (PWEH-bloh) A Hopi village made of many adobe houses that are connected.

reservation (reh-zer-VAY-shun) An area of land that the government has set aside for Native Americans to live on.

traditional (truh-DISH-un-ul) Doing things the way that a group of people has done them for a long time.

tribe (TRYB) A group of people that forms a community and shares the same traditions.

turquoise (TER-koyz) A blue-green stone that many Native Americans use to make jewelry.

Index